SUBMARINES

BY
COMMANDER JEFF TALL OBE RN

What Is a Submarine?

A submarine is a ship designed to travel long distances below the surface of the water. It is used for exploration and commercial purposes, but the submarine is most commonly recognized as a military fighting machine designed to carry and fire torpedoes and missiles. From earliest times, ships have been used in conflicts, and the submarine offers the threat of attack from an unseen fighting machine. Today's submarines are designed with a streamlined double hull; ballast tanks (the spaces between the inner and outer hull into which seawater is flooded when diving and then forced out by air when surfacing); horizontal rudders (hydroplanes) which angle the ship up and down; and a propulsion system to drive it through the water. In short . . . a mechanical whale.

THE MINISUBMARINE

Electrically driven minisubmarines are regularly used for commercial purposes. Engineers are able to check underwater equipment such as oil and gas pipelines and scientists can explore the deepest parts of the oceans. These submarines usually have a crew of two who use searchlights and underwater video to help them navigate. Some are also fitted with a robot arm to retrieve items from the seabed.

THE DITTY BOX

Because of the need to carry as many torpedoes as possible, along with listening devices and other machinery, there is not a lot of room for the crew inside a submarine. All that a sailor could take onboard early submarines was his ditty box, in which he kept his valuables, such as letters from home and photographs. There was not even enough room for a change of clothing; this, combined with a shortage of fresh water, meant that after a short time things got very smelly indeed. Because everyone smelled the same, this did not matter . . . until they stepped ashore!

SUBMARINES AT THE MOVIES

Submarines are popular in films, mainly because of the mystery of what happens in a steel tube full of men and machinery living and working hundreds of feet beneath the sea. Recent examples are *The Hunt for Red October* and *Crimson Tide*. Perhaps the movie that caught the popular imagination the most was *Das Boote*, the story of a WWII German U-boat crew who, in the space of four hours on screen, suffered every disaster that could have been experienced by any submarine!

THE CONTROL ROOM

The Control Room is the "brain" of the submarine, and it is from here that the captain issues his orders: which direction to steer; how fast to go; what depth to keep; which target to search for; what weapons to keep at instant readiness; when to send a transmission, etc. Usually half of the crew would be on "watch" or otherwise busy, while the other half would be eating or relaxing. Whether awake or asleep, everyone is constantly ready to react to danger.

THE SHAPE OF THINGS TO COME

This model shows the important external features of a submarine: the ballast tanks are attached to the circular hull for diving and surfacing; the planes and rudder are used for horizontal and vertical control; the conning tower is used for stability and housing the periscopes; the sleek shape of the bow (front) cuts through the water and carries the torpedo tubes.

THE "JOLLY ROGER"

In 1901, submarines were not popular with nations that "ruled the waves" with their battleships because of the threat of a surprise attack. One opponent to their introduction into the Royal Navy was Admiral Arthur Wilson, who said that any submariner captured should be "hanged as a pirate." A few years later, a young British submarine captain raised the pirate flag of a white skull and crossbones (the "Jolly Roger") as a badge of honor after he had sunk an enemy cruiser. From that day on, the flag became the emblem of British submarines; every crew made their own flag to be flown after successful patrols. The symbols on the flag to the right shows successes in mining, gun actions, and sinking enemy ships.

Early Submarines

*I*nventors and scientists of early generations were faced with an enormous challenge trying to unlock and conquer the secrets of the oceans. As they put the first tentative toe into the water, they had little understanding of the element and its physical properties: e.g., how it changes with depth, how it varies in density between fresh and salt water, and the treacherous subsurface currents. Through a variety of dangerous experiments, they slowly but surely pushed the frontiers of knowledge forward. Counteracting the craft's buoyancy and getting it beneath the surface, keeping water out, refreshing the air to avoid suffocating the crew, and propelling the craft underwater were all practical problems that had to be overcome with only the most basic materials of wood and leather available to work with. Nevertheless, they persevered, and by the eighteenth century goatskin had given way to metal hoops for strength, and the oar had been replaced by a crankshaft and propeller for propulsion. The submarine design that we know today was beginning to take shape.

THE FIRST OCEAN VOYAGE

Simon Lake's *Argonaut* (USA) can claim to have been the first submarine ever to make an ocean voyage. In 1898 it traveled under its own power through November storms from Norfolk, Virginia, to New York—a remarkable feat. From the *Argonaut* Lake developed a military version, the *Protector*.

THE TURTLE ATTACKS

The first submarine attack in naval history took place in New York harbor, in 1776, during the American War of Independence. The *Turtle*, designed by David Bushell, came remarkably close to sinking its target. It carried a detachable mine which was intended to be drilled into the wooden bottom of the British target ship, HMS *Eagle*. Because of an impenetrable metal plate on the underside of the ship, the mission was not a success.

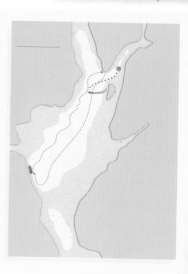

NINE BRAVE MEN

The first submarine to sink another warship was the CSS *Hunley*. In 1864, during the American Civil War, it successfully attacked the USS *Housatonic*. Eight men and the captain were cramped into a tiny space, turning a long crankshaft. They paid a heavy price for their efforts.

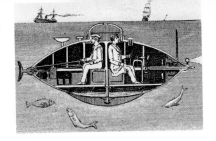

THE *HUNLEY'S* TORPEDO

The torpedo was a large mine on a harpoon spar that had to be rammed against the target's wooden side. The explosion should have occurred once the submarine had backed away; unfortunately, it went off too early. The *Hunley* was swamped by the blast and sank with all its crew.

THE LITTLE *GOUBET*

This tiny submarine was the first to be powered by electricity. The basic concept was that it could be carried by a battleship and set down within its range of target. Although beset by problems, it had sufficient merit to be bought by the Brazilian navy.

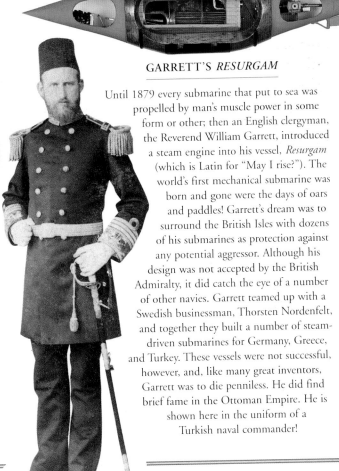

GARRETT'S *RESURGAM*

Until 1879 every submarine that put to sea was propelled by man's muscle power in some form or other; then an English clergyman, the Reverend William Garrett, introduced a steam engine into his vessel, *Resurgam* (which is Latin for "May I rise?"). The world's first mechanical submarine was born and gone were the days of oars and paddles! Garrett's dream was to surround the British Isles with dozens of his submarines as protection against any potential aggressor. Although his design was not accepted by the British Admiralty, it did catch the eye of a number of other navies. Garrett teamed up with a Swedish businessman, Thorsten Nordenfelt, and together they built a number of steam-driven submarines for Germany, Greece, and Turkey. These vessels were not successful, however, and, like many great inventors, Garrett was to die penniless. He did find brief fame in the Ottoman Empire. He is shown here in the uniform of a Turkish naval commander!

SUBMARINES IN ANCIENT TIMES

Medieval manuscripts tell of Alexander the Great being lowered in a glass barrel, in which he remained on the bottom of the sea for some time, and on surfacing described the wonderful things he had seen. He is reputed to have used manned submersibles in Tyre harbor in 332 B.C. in order to defend his ships from divers who were attempting to cut their anchor ropes. But it was to be another eighteen centuries before the idea of submersible ships was discussed again.

HOLLAND 1

In 1901 the British Navy adopted the design of the *Holland* Class for its first experiment[al] submarines. *Holland 1* is pictured here at se[a] with seven of the eight crew members on th[e] casing (upper deck). Note the lack of a conni[ng] tower—it is easy to see why these little submari[nes] suffered flooding during a storm!

A STEEL FISH

In 1898 a report in the *New York Journal* read *"STEEL FISH WITH REVOLVING TAIL WILL PROTECT OUR HARBOR—The Holland Submarine Terror, the Newest Wonder of Naval Science, Which Lives and Swims Under Water and Noiselessly and Unseen Creeps Up Under an Enemy's Side, Hurling Into It Thunderbolts of Dynamite from Its Torpedo Guns."*

CONTROL ROOM

This cutaway of *Holland 1* shows that a great deal of technical progress was made in only three years from *Holland*'s first design. Officers in the control room steered the submarine when it was submerged.

INSIDE THE FISH

The reporter from the *New York Journal* drew a number of images of the craft, which clearly show that the earliest form of navigation was the captain looking out of a porthole, standing on a soapbox, with a member of the crew having to lie down to get past him.

THE PROPULSION TRAIN

The gasoline engine could only power the submarine on the surface. It was connected to the motor, shaft, and propeller to drive the submarine along at about 10 knots. The engine also charged the battery, which provided the energy to turn the motor when the submarine was submerged. A speed of 7 knots could be reached and maintained for about five hours before the battery was exhausted.

The USS *Holland*

The first wholly successful submarine in history was the USS *Holland,* the U.S. Navy's first submarine (bought in 1900). Because it was powered by one of the recently invented internal combustion engines burning gasoline, the submarine's inventor, John Philip Holland, was able to make his design smaller and much more efficient than its steam-driven equivalent. This engine was coupled to an electric generator to recharge the batteries that supplied the electric motor, which propelled the submarine when it was submerged. In the bow was a launch tube for one of the new Whitehead torpedoes. Most important of all, Holland knew how to make a submarine behave properly, with the capability of submerging or surfacing rapidly, and of remaining level when traveling at depth under water.

THE FIRST DESIGNS

John Philip Holland, the inventor of the modern submarine, was an American of Irish birth. He was a brilliant designer and spent many of his early years building submarines that were intended to attack ships in New York Harbor! In 1898 he created the blueprint for the mother of all submarines afloat today. The efficient use of the internal combustion engine and electric motor to power the craft produced the first successful long-distance submarine, which was to become the USS *Holland.*

THE TORPEDO TUBE

The great advance in torpedo technology occurred in 1868 when the British engineer, Sir Robert Whitehead, fired the world's first locomotive torpedo. He was also the grandfather of the Von Trapp Singers *(The Sound of Music)*! The torpedo was expelled from the tube by high-pressure air. It only had a range of about 1,000 feet (300 meters), so the submarine had to get close to its target to be successful.

THE MOTHER SHIP

This model of *Holland 1* shows a remarkable resemblance to a whale, and explains why the design was so successful. Although submarines have become bigger and more powerful, the basic principles have remained the same.

Up to 1913

The French were great submarine pioneers but, because they began their design program many years before J. P. Holland in the United States, they were unable to adapt quickly to new technology. In 1901 they introduced twenty small submarines as defense mobiles for a number of ports. Their gasoline-driven engines soon proved hazardous, so the submarines had to recharge their batteries when at port, greatly limiting their range. They carried their two torpedoes on the outside, unlike other submarines which carried theirs internally.

Submarining in the early twentieth century was a rough and ready, rude, and ruthless way of life, whose impact on the social structure of the British navy was revolutionary. Never before had officers and men served and lived so closely together, sharing the inherent dangers and also the crudest sanitary arrangements (buckets!). Of danger there were many—exploding gasoline engines; collision; flooding—and submariners in many navies lost their lives in accidents. However, technology and safety (but not comfort) slowly improved: gasoline engines gave way to diesel (a safe fuel); internal bulkheads were introduced to limit flooding; higher conning towers provided protection against rough seas; the size and strength of hulls increased; periscopes, and thus the safety lookout, were vastly improved. By the outbreak of World War I, the submarine, though viewed as a defensive weapon, was established in every major fleet worldwide.

THREE WHITE MICE

One of the most dangerous exhaust products of a gasoline engine is carbon monoxide, which has no smell. Exhaust from the engine was designed to be expelled through a mast, but it would often creep into the boat threatening to asphyxiate the crew. A mouse, which has only a small body weight would quickly react to a leak by becoming unconscious. If one collapsed, the submarine quickly surfaced for fresh air.

JAPANESE OFFICER'S CEREMONIAL SWORD

Despite the crude conditions onboard submarines, all the crew would have a full uniform to wear when ashore or on ceremonial occasions. The Imperial Japanese Navy, which introduced *Holland* Class submarines in 1904, was no exception. The rise of the Japanese navy was remarkable, reaching in decades a level of skill which had taken many other nations centuries to achieve. Always at the forefront of technology, Japan, during the Russo-Japanese war of 1904–1905, was the first nation in history to successfully launch a torpedo against an enemy ship.

YES TO SUBMARINES

When the submarine was first introduced into the United States there was a lot of general unease about its presence. Lieutenant Larry H. Caldwell (seen here with his crew on board the first American submarine [in June 1901]) was a respected officer who could foresee the future strengths of the submarine. He became a pioneer for the acceptance of such a fighting force into the navy despite being faced with strong opposition.

FAST AND DANGEROUS

In 1916, the British Royal Navy introduced a submarine capable of providing support to surface warships. Known as the "fleet escort" submarine, it was designated the K-class and 18 were built. In order to be effective, the submarine had to be able to travel at 24 knots when surfaced. This could not be achieved by diesel engines, so steam was used to power the engines, making them the fastest submarines in the world until nuclear-powered submarines were invented. The Ks were the most hazardous submarines ever introduced and eight were destroyed, killing a large number of their crews.

HOME COMFORTS

Of all "men-of-war," the submarine is the least self-supporting when not actively employed at sea. Every aspect of life on board points to the necessity for a base for both the boat and the crew when they are in harbor. Shore bases and depot ships serve this purpose. The *Acheron*, a German ship, was a typical example of an early depot ship, which could provide the basic amenities of a bed and a bath. Later depot ships could also go to sea and provide mobile dockyard support.

INSIDE A SUBMARINE

This photograph shows the need for comfort when not at sea! Several men would call this cramped space home, and "cheek-to-cheek" with the torpedoes they would eat, sleep, write their letters home and generally conduct their lives. Privacy was nonexistent, and the need to get along with each other was of paramount importance. The torpedo tubes in the background were an ever-present statement of the job they were expected to do, and constantly reminded them of the danger they faced together. At "Action Stations" the table and seat lockers would be folded away.

The First World War

*I*t was during W.W. I amid great controversy that the submarine came of age as a weapon system. Great Britain had always relied on the sea-lanes for vital supplies, so the Germans used their U-boats against Great Britain's merchant shipping to starve the country into submission. This proved that the submarine could be used as an effective weapon. Between 1914 and 1918, the most successful German U-boat, *U-35,* managed to sink 324 merchant ships. Then, in 1917, the Allies started to sail their merchant ships in convoys protected by a warship escort. This greatly reduced the number of ships lost through submarine attack. The convoy system and the entry of the United States into the war kept the essential lifeline across the Atlantic open.

At this time, there was no means available to detect a submarine other than from visual lookout, since ASDIC (sound detection) was invented after the war.

A DANGEROUS LIFE

The mine was the greatest hazard faced by a submarine crew. Unseen, undetectable, and unpredictable, this devastating weapon accounted for hundreds of submariners' lives during both World Wars. The young men from HMS *E34* in the photo above not only suffered extreme discomfort at sea, but their lives were snuffed out in an instant in 1918 when they touched the horn of an enemy mine in the North Sea.

SENDING MESSAGES

Until the introduction of wireless telegraphy into submarines in 1916, the signalman had to rely on semaphore flags, pigeon post, and the Aldis Lamp as methods of exchanging messages. Wireless telegraphy, with an eventual radius of 100 miles, provided up-to-date information from ashore.

TURKISH BLUNDERBUSS

British submarines operated extensively during the Dardanelles' campaign against the Turks, who were German allies. One misty morning a lone Turkish fisherman came across HMS *E12* charging her batteries on the surface. In sheer fright he let loose his blunderbuss (a muzzle-loading gun) at the grey monster. His punishment was the loss of his gun—but he was given a brandy in compensation and set free.

THE LOOKOUT

When traveling on the surface, it was essential for a submarine to maintain a vigilant lookout in order to find its target and avoid being surprised. In rough weather this was a cold and wet duty. These lookouts on the bridge of a U-boat, dressed in raincoats, are well protected from the elements in order to conduct their search of the horizon. One of their shipmates has just finished his period of watch and is escaping to relative comfort below. In the cat and mouse game of submarining, it was kill or be killed—with no room for error.

THE *LUSITANIA*

The event that brought home the appalling consequences of submarine warfare was the sinking of the Cunard Liner, *Lusitania*, by the German submarine *U-20* in May 1915. Nearly 1,200 lives were lost, including many women and children. This grave error of judgment weakened the United States' resolve to remain neutral in the war, since a number of the *Lusitania*'s passengers were American. A propaganda medal was struck in Germany to celebrate the "success."

THE FACE OF A SHARK

Submarines had to enter dry dock occasionally to have their underwater fittings overhauled. The two port torpedo tubes of this German *U-162* can be seen with the bow caps open, and behind them are the bow shutters that completed the streamlining of the hull when they were shut. The serrated device on the bow was designed to cut mooring wires of any mines encountered. From this angle the submarine resembles more of a shark than a whale.

NAVIGATION

The sextant was a device used in aerial navigation. Its basic principle was to measure angles of the sun, stars, and planets, which, when converted into bearing lines, provided a position on the earth's surface. It was often the only means of navigating, but if there was constant cloud cover a submarine could go for days without being able to "fix" its position. This could, and occasionally did, have disastrous consequences, particularly with respect to avoiding known minefields, or straying out of its defined patrol area where it was safe from friendly fire.

THE FIGUREHEAD

Even when not at war, submarines are still very dangerous ships to operate. Since one mistake can be disastrous for all, comradeship and excellence in performance are vital for safe and efficient operation. Thus submariners are fiercely proud of their ship and devoted to its well-being. One way of expressing this pride is through the ceremonial flagstaff figurehead erected when the submarine is in harbor. The magnificent example shown to the right was that of HMS *Poseidon*, which unfortunately collided with a ship in 1931, killing twenty of its crew.

EAST AND WEST

Dependent on the sea for trade, Britain and Japan have much in common. There was close cooperation for a short time between the two navies. For example, the design of the Japanese *RO* Class submarine was based on the British *L* Class.

BIG GUNS

This submarine, HMS *M1*, armed with a monster 12-inch gun, was intended to pop up to the surface when the enemy was sighted, and then bombard him until the fleet battleships joined in. It was assumed that the submarine's low profile would keep it safe from retaliation. Fortunately, the theory was never tested!

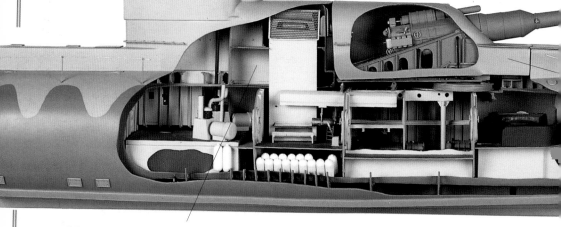

PROVIDING AN ESCORT

The concept of an escort submarine working very closely with surface ships of the fleet meant that the submarine had to travel at 24 knots on the surface to keep up with destroyers, a speed impossible for diesel engines to achieve. So steam propulsion was introduced, with oil-fired boilers producing the required heat. This made life very complicated for the crews, and many submarines were lost by accident.

THE MIGHTY FRENCH *SURCOUF*

Designed as a raider against merchant ships, this was the biggest and most famous submarine in the world in her day. She had everything: the greatest displacement, a range of 10,000 miles, two 8-inch guns, 22 torpedoes, and a seaplane! In W.W. II this monster fought gallantly for the Allies, but was sunk by accident in 1942.

Between the Wars

Great Britain's immediate reaction to the submarine at the end of W.W. I was an attempt to get it banned! Her allies did not agree, although a limit was put on the total number of submarines in each navy. A common conclusion reached by naval analysts was that the submarine could be a crucial weapon in any future conflict, but it needed to be more effective with increased range, better weapons, and higher speeds. Designers met the challenge with a variety of submarine shapes and sizes, many of which were impracticable and often dangerous to the crews. In addition, every major maritime nation also built standard submarines. Germany, too, was making progress in the development of more powerful submarines. Hitler was not slow in instigating the means to produce high-quality submarines. This was something the Allies were going to discover at their own cost.

RECREATION

Obviously there was not enough room onboard to enjoy much in way of recreation, so games such as checkers, dominoes, and card games were dominant features of mess life. All these apparently innocent games were played with cutthroat intensity, and to be an individual champion onboard provided a status that enhanced even the lowliest rank. A great treat and distraction would be the nightly movie, even though the projector was forever running out of oil or breaking down!

ROVING EYES

The gun turret was replaced in HMS *M2* by a hanger and a small recoverable aircraft that was to act as "eyes" to the fleet. This conversion recognized the part that aircraft would play in future maritime conflicts. Both the *M1* and *M2* were lost in accidents.

FRESH FOOD

Fresh food such as vegetables and fruit lasted for only a few days in a submarine before it spoiled. The diet on board was dominated by meals that were either dehydrated or out of a can, and it was remarkable how many variations could be made out of spam! Extra rations of orange juice were supplied to maintain vitamin levels, and bread was baked overnight. But a banana, no matter how old, was always a treat!

World War II...

While Hitler and his Nazis were determined to overrun continental Europe, they wanted nothing from Great Britain but to be left alone. Indeed, they were convinced that if they allowed "Britannia to rule the waves," they could avoid a general conflict. Thus Germany maintained only a small navy, whereas her army and air force were built up significantly for the invasions ahead. When war with Britain did break out, the Germans soon realized that naval engagements in the classical sense were out of the question, and only by attacking merchant vessels could they make their presence felt at sea. The early years of the Battle of the Atlantic, despite convoys and ASDIC-fitted escorts, saw the success of the U-boats, but not for long.

GERMAN COMMAND

Admiral Karl Doenitz assumed command of the U-boat force in 1935. He foresaw the forthcoming war with Britain and wanted 300 U-boats. Fortunately for the Allies, he did not get them. He made the best of what he had by concentrating them in "wolf packs," and succeeded in sinking hundreds of merchant vessels.

DEADLY CARGO

The deadly cargo of torpedoes can be seen in this Type VIIb U-boat. A total of twelve would be carried, and the commanding officer would endeavor to make every weapon count by getting in close to the target, crippling it with one torpedo, and finishing it off with his gun. The invention of radar and the introduction of long range Coastal Command aircraft swung the battle against the U-boat. By the end of the war, over 750 U-boats were destroyed with a huge loss of life.

U-BOAT PEN

A tug boat is guiding the Japanese submarine *I29* into the safety of a German reinforced concrete, bomb-proof U-boat pen in Bordeaux, France. Japanese submarines made a number of long-distance trips to collect secret equipment from their German allies.

THE ROYAL MARINE HEROES

An important task for British submarines was landing and recovering agents and special forces. One of the most famous exploits was the Special Boat Service's highly successful raid on Bordeaux when they sank several ships with limpet mines. Their shallow boats were launched from HMS *Tuna*. Ten extremely brave Royal Marines took part in the operation— eight were killed.

THE KNIGHT'S CROSS

This was a German medal awarded for extreme bravery. An early winner in U-boats was Gunter Prien, the captain of *U-47*. In October 1939 he pulled off one of the most spectacular exploits of the war when he penetrated British defenses at Scapa Flow, Orkney Islands, and sank the battleship HMS *Royal Oak*. *U-47* was sunk in 1941 by HMS *Verity* and *Wolverine*.

J-47'S BRIDGE

Until 1944 (when some boats were fitted with the "Schnorkel") U-boats had to surface for transit to their patrol areas. During transit they were at high risk of attack from the air, so the bridge would be crowded with lookouts and antiaircraft gunners!

JAPANESE SUBMARINES

Despite having the best torpedo in the world (the Long Lance), Japanese submarines were never allowed to make an effective contribution to the overall Battle of the Pacific. They were not used as an independent offensive arm. Instead they were fleet escorts, as they had been in World War I, and the Japanese navy wasted their energies by building huge submarines capable of little else than serving as communication ships, or tankers for flying boats.

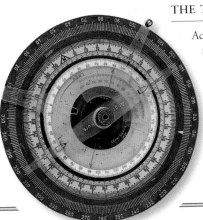

LONG-DISTANCE TRAVEL

U-boats were employed to attack merchant ships, so they had to travel long distances to intercept Allied convoys sailing across the Atlantic. The convoys sailed as far north as possible to try to escape detection. This made the U-boats' job difficult, but their range of 6,500 miles meant that their prey was always within reach.

THE TORPEDO CALCULATOR

Achieving a torpedo hit against a moving target was a complicated business. The most important factor was knowing when to fire so that the weapon intercepted the target track at the right moment. Adding torpedo angles and fans to cover range, direction, and speed inaccuracies often made it too difficult for the captain to calculate accurately.

AN AWARD FOR MALTA

Malta was crucial to the conduct of the campaign against Rommel's Afrika Corps. It was home to the Royal Air Force bomber and fighter aircraft and the *Fighting Tenth* submarine squadron. Despite being pulverized by German bombers both by day and night, the starving islanders resolutely refused to surrender. In recognition of their supreme courage, King George VI of England bestowed on them the highest civilian award for bravery, The George Cross.

HANGING ON

It took luck to survive a submarine attack. There was often no time to launch lifeboats, and men would cling onto any wreckage that floated, without food and water and for days on end. They were the unsung heroes of the war.

A HOMECOMING CELEBRATION

This cake was baked by the mother of telegraph operator Albert Hamilton-Smith to celebrate his return home. Tragically, his submarine, HMS *P33*, was lost with all hands off Tripoli in August 1941. The cake was kept in his memory.

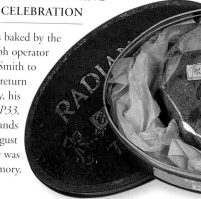

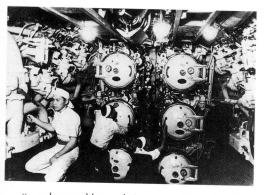

TORPEDOES AWAY!

This torpedo space of a large Japanese submarine contained six tubes. At one end of the tubes would be bow caps, which would be opened as the submarine prepared to launch. When the captain ordered "Fire," high-pressure air would expel the weapons. When the torpedoes moved, triggers in the tubes would start their engines. Thereafter they were on their own, following predetermined calculated courses toward their target.

INFERIOR MACHINES

Italian submarines operated in the North Atlantic under the command of Admiral Doenitz. They were technically inferior to his U-boats and he was so disappointed with their performance that he moved over 60 of his own precious submarines into the Mediterranean to counter the British fleet. This in turn weakened his campaign against Allied merchant shipping.

THE *REGIA MARINA*

This Italian submarine surrendered in September 1943. Italy entered the war with 100 submarines, but at the time of its surrender 86 of them had been sunk or captured.

...World War II

As in the North Atlantic, submarines played an important, often vital, role in other areas of the war. In the Mediterranean, British submarines operating from Malta and Alexandria fought a desperate battle against General Rommel's supply lines to North Africa. In conjunction with the Royal Air Force, they deprived Rommel of half of what he needed by way of reinforcements, and stopped him from reaching the Suez Canal. In East Asia the Japanese, having conquered all the western islands of the Pacific, found themselves subjected to an onslaught by the U.S. Submarine Service, against which they had little effective defense. British submarines were also active with the Americans from the Allied base in Fremantle, western Australia. Although losses were much less than those of Germany, a significant proportion of Allied submariners (including French, Dutch, Polish, Soviets, and Greeks) lost their lives, many of them to the deadliest of W.W. II antisubmarine weapons—the mine.

A PRESENT FROM MOIRA

Every Royal Navy submarine had a "trophy" that was closely related to its name. For example, HMS *Tallyho* had a hunting horn, HMS *Turpin* had a flintlock pistol, and HMS *Totem* had a totem pole. HMS *Tiptoe* not only had a ballet dancer on its badge, but also boasted a pair of ballet shoes presented by the famous ballerina Moira Shearer. Miss Shearer had worn them during the making of the film *The Red Shoes*. HMS *Tiptoe* has the distinction of being the last submarine to sink an enemy ship in W.W. II by torpedo when, in August 1945, it sent a Japanese freighter to the bottom of the Pacific.

THE SUBMARINE GUN

Being small, Italian submarines could carry more shells for the gun than torpedoes, so it was an ideal weapon house against lightly armed opposition that didn't have aircraft cover.

AN EXCEPTIONAL VOLUNTEER

The tankard belonged to HMS *Storm*, the only submarine ever to have been commanded by an officer in the Royal Navy Volunteer Reserve. The RNVR consisted of men and women who were not in a maritime profession at the outbreak of war, so to be given command of a submarine meant that you were an exceptional individual. The man concerned was Lieutenant Commander Edward Young DSO DSC RNVR.

How a Submarine Works

A submarine can dive to great depths as determined by the strength of the pressure hull. Once submerged, the crew depends on a mass of electronics and air purification equipment to survive. Diesel-powered submarines need to surface regularly to recharge batteries, but nuclear submarines can cruise at depth indefinitely. Communication is important and messages can be sent and received via satellites. Low-frequency radio waves are also used to avoid detection. In order to "hear" what is going on, the submerged submarine uses sonar. Modern submarines are fitted with a system called the Ship's Inertial Navigation System (SINS). A set of gyroscopes record the submarine's movements and a computer calculates its exact position. This system is entirely electronic and very accurate.

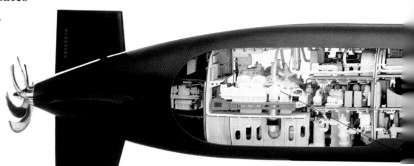

SUBMARINE CONTROL

When on the surface, the submarine sits on a cushion of air in its ballast tanks in a condition known as "positive buoyancy." Because of the ship's shape it can be very uncomfortable on board in a rough sea!

Air is released from the ballast tanks by opening main vents and letting water in. The added weight of water now makes it "negatively buoyant." "Down she goes."

Ballast tanks

Hydroplanes

Trimming tanks

To surface, high-pressure air is blown into the ballast tanks (with the main vents shut) to expel water. This restores "positive buoyancy," and "up she comes."

Once at depth, the body weight is adjusted to the outside density of the sea. This is known as "neutral buoyancy." Hydroplanes maintain the angle.

To remain level, trimming tanks are emptied or filled to compensate for body weight or density changes caused by depth alterations or discharges of water.

SUBMARINE "EYES"

Every submarine has an "attack" and a "search" periscope, which are raised and lowered by hydraulic power. The periscopes are the "eyes" of the submarine, and are manned when the submarine is at periscope depth. Common features are a target "ranging facility" and high/low magnification.

The "attack" periscope has a single eyepiece, and has a much narrower head at the top, which makes it harder to detect by radar or the naked eye. It is used for close-in work against a target.

The "search" periscope has two eye pieces for good horizon scanning, and a bigger top end. It also has features such as low-light television, infrared detection, camera facility, radar warning, and satellite communications capability.

A BREATH OF FRESH AIR

In order to get fresh air underwater, a submarine has an electrolysis machine which splits water into oxygen and hydrogen gasses. An electric current passes through the water creating fresh oxygen. Soda lime removes hydrogen.

ELECTRIC ENGINES

Depending on the design of the submarine, propulsion is provided by either an electric motor or steam turbine. Electricity is provided in the same way, and is fed around the submarine by a "ring main." Off this ring main is tapped a whole variety of differing electric voltages and frequencies to drive the myriad equipment on board.

UP PERISCOPE

This is the sight that the captain would see of a frigate at about 1,000 yards. The bow wave indicates that it is traveling at about 15 knots. The periscope would only be exposed for about five seconds, and submarine speed would be kept very low to avoid making a wake in the water. Even so, this is too close for comfort!

DOWN, DOWN, DOWN

The blasts of "steam" surrounding this *Porpoise* Class submarine were in fact plumes of air being driven out of her ballast tanks as water rushes in. The ship was conducting a test dive before going on patrol, the purpose of which was to ensure that the submarine was watertight after major work on its hull fittings.

Attack and Defense

Slowly but surely the idea of the submarine as a defensive weapon changed; it was finally acknowledged as the perfect platform to deliver a mighty blow under a cloak of stealth and surprise. So hulls became bigger and weapons more powerful. Short-range torpedoes of half a mile gave way to the modern torpedo with a range of more than 15 miles. The sea-skimming antiship missile, which can travel about 70 miles, has replaced the deck gun. A land attack is possible with the development of the Tomahawk cruise missile (range: 2,000 miles plus), which has taken over from the huge ballistic missiles such as Polaris and Trident. Defensively the submarine has come a long way too—today it is fast, quiet, deep diving, very hard to detect, and can stay under water for months.

LOW-LEVEL MISSILES

An excellent antiship missile is the Sub-Harpoon, which is fitted to all U.S. Navy and Royal Navy attack submarines; it is seen here emerging from its launch capsule. It has a range in excess of 70 miles, and homes in on its target through the radar set in its nose. It skims the sea and approaches its target at a very low level. It is therefore very difficult to detect and shoot down.

MAKING WEAPONS

The first torpedo factory in the world was in Fiume, Austria, where Sir Robert Whitehead, the torpedo pioneer, worked for the government. The modern equivalent of these late 19th-century workers, who in turn, were working at the forefront of technology, are dressed in white, dustproof, antistatic coveralls and surrounded by computer wizardry!

THE INTERCONTINENTAL BALLISTIC MISSILE

The purpose of these missiles is to deter aggression by a potential enemy who may be tempted to strike the first blow with weapons of mass destruction. In order for deterrence to work, retaliation against an aggressor must be effective and guaranteed. The submarine is an excellent platform on which to deploy these "last resort" weapons since its position can be kept secret until the last moment. It can stay on the move, and can remain at sea, for extended periods. When fired, missile warheads leave the earth's atmosphere for a short time before plunging onto their target, making them almost impossible to defend against.

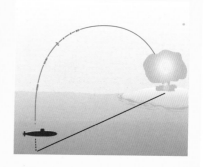

TORPEDO ATTACK

This picture shows the devastating effect of a torpedo against a large frigate. Modern torpedoes are fitted with a number of fuses (or initiating devices). In this case it was the magnetic fuse that reacted, causing the torpedo to explode beneath the target. This created a vortex (hole) in the sea, and with the keel of the target ship unsupported, its back was broken. The other major type of fuse is impact, designed to set off the torpedo explosive when it physically strikes its target.

A SUBMARINE'S EARS

Just as the periscopes are the "eyes" of the submarine, its sonar sets are its "ears." Operators man the sets, and they are trained to listen for and recognize the many different sounds that fill the oceans.

TACTICAL WEAPONS

The modern torpedo is an awesome weapon that, unlike the missile, will quickly sink the target it strikes. The firing submarine guides it by wire to the vicinity of the target, and when it is close enough the torpedo will tell its guider that it is in contact. It will then home in on its target and attack, giving the target little time to take action.

MAIN ELEMENTS OF THE TACTICAL WEAPON SYSTEM

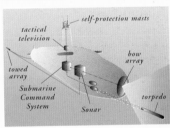

The total weapon system enables a submarine to detect, classify, approach, and fire at its target. Detection will be achieved on sonar, and classification will be made by recognizing the "fingerprint" of the target. Because submarines try only to listen, rather than transmit the traditional sonar "ping" (which would give its presence away), it has to work very hard to determine when the target is within range of its torpedoes. Once the captain is certain that he has a satisfactory solution, he will launch his weapon, giving his prey the minimum amount of time to react.

SUBMARINE HUNTERS

One of the most effective submarine hunters, apart from another submarine, is the helicopter. Because it is very agile, it is also very unpredictable, so a submarine trying to escape from its active sonar is never quite sure where it will pop up next! It is particularly effective when working in pairs. A helicopter can carry two lightweight torpedoes, so it packs quite a punch.

Burton Daily Mail

SUBMARINE MISSING IN CHANNEL

Aircraft and Ships Engaged in Widespread Search

The Cruel Sea

The waves of the sea are the only gravestones of many thousands of men who went down with their submarines and whose bodies have never been recovered. Up to 1995, a total of 1,761 submarines were lost, of which 313 were lost by accident or error. These accidents happened through a whole range of causes: structural faults, collision, human error, and battery explosions, to name just a few. It was often the case that, after such an accident, at least some of the crew would manage to survive, often for a considerable time. The tragedy of the cruel sea was that very few managed to escape from their metal prison. It was not until there was a greater understanding of the human body's reactions under extremes of pressure that equipment and techniques were developed that allowed a reasonable chance of survival. On both sides of the Atlantic experimentation began to find the means of helping crew members escape from submarines.

MISSING SUBMARINES

Submarines carry an Emergency Indicator Buoy, which, when released by survivors inside the hull, pops to the surface and transmits an SOS. This both announces that a disaster has occurred and acts as a homing beacon. Such was the calamity that sank HMS *Affray*; its buoy was not released, and it took six weeks to find the ship.

A FLAMMABLE WETSUIT

This bulky apparatus was patented in 1907. However, the chemical it used to produce oxygen, sodium peroxide, caught fire if it got wet! Fortunately, Robert Davis, a mining safety engineer and diving equipment pioneer, was soon to develop a smaller device which also doubled as a life jacket.

A LETTER FROM LIEUTENANT SAKUMA

Japanese submarine *No. 6* sank in April 1910. While the captain, Lieutenant Sakuma, sat waiting for death, he wrote a remarkable letter to his emperor, which was recovered later by a salvage team. It reads in part,
To His Majesty: I am very sorry that, owing to my carelessness, I have sunk His Majesty's submarine and killed the officers and men under my orders, but I am glad they have all faithfully discharged their duties . . . Sire, I entreat you to look after the families of my men so that they do not starve; this is the only thing that bothers me.

A GREAT DISASTER

The Royal Navy's greatest submarine disaster occurred in June 1939 when, during trials in Liverpool Bay, HMS *Thetis* sank with 103 men on board, 50 more than usual. Due to a series of mishaps and misjudgments, only four escaped, despite the fact that the submarine was visible throughout the drama. The remaining 99 men died when the oxygen in the submarine ran out. Their epitaph might read, *Death on the battlefield beneath the blue sky is one thing . . . but death in a submarine, carried downward in a steel tube that is also a vault, without another glimpse of the sun, is another.*

TO THE RESCUE

After World War II the United States Navy began to work on the design of a craft to rescue crews from great depths. The end result was a minisubmarine, the Deep Submergence Rescue Vessel (DSRV). The DSRV is carried to the scene of the distressed submarine by another

submarine, which then acts as the rescue ship. The DSRV then connects itself to the escape hatch of the troubled submarine, allowing survivors to come on board. It then ferries the rescued crew back to the waiting rescue vessel.

SUNK BY FRIENDLY FIRE

The most tragic fate that can befall a submarine is to be sunk by friendly forces. The submarine shown was rammed and sunk by an Allied frigate, before being salvaged and dragged into shallow water. One of the reasons that submarines had huge numbers and letters painted on their conning towers was to stop them from being bombed by "friendly" aircraft. Unfortunately, this did not work on many occasions.

THE ESCAPE SUIT

Down to depths of 600 feet it is possible to survive using an escape suit. Dressed in his suit, the survivor climbs into the submarine's escape tower and then shoots to the surface like a cork. Even in the coldest and roughest conditions, the highly visible orange suit acts like a life raft, and keeps the survivor alive, possibly for up to five days, until help arrives.

UNIFORM OF A CHARIOTEER

In the early days, equipment used by the crew of the Chariots was crude and dangerous, and was simply a conversion of submarine escape equipment, ill suited to the rigors of physical exertion. Eventually, specialist equipment, such as this helmet, was developed and they emerged looking like modern frogmen.

ROOM FOR TWO

Chariots had a crew of two. It was the Number 1's job to navigate and control the craft; the Number 2 cleared away obstructions and placed the explosive charge against the target. This charge was in fact the chariot's detachable nose.

THE ITALIAN HUMAN TORPEDO

The Italians were the great pioneers of the Midget Submarine and had built their first prototype in 1935. Their outstandingly brave team of volunteers achieved one of the most astonishing feats of World War II. In December 1941, three human torpedoes sank the battleships HMS *Queen Elizabeth* and *Valiant* in Alexandria Harbor in Egypt. This could have changed the course of the war. However, the water was shallow, so both ships settled on the bottom with their upper part still intact, which allowed them to simulate readiness for sea by emitting funnel smoke. Because the Italian crews had been captured, the Italian High Command never realized how close they were to naval dominance of the Mediterranean.

SMALL BUT DEADLY

It was the British who produced the most effective Midget Submarine of the war: the four-man, diesel-electric powered X craft. Introduced in 1943, their armament consisted of two large side cargoes of high explosive, releasable from inside the submarine, which were designed to be laid under the target. Four Victoria Crosses, the highest award for gallantry, were awarded to British crews who successfully crippled the German battleship *Tirpitz* in a Norwegian fjord, and the Japanese cruiser *Takao* in Singapore Harbor.

THE JAPANESE *HA*-BOAT

Along with 27 large submarines, five torpedo-armed Japanese *HA*-boats took part in the raid on Pearl Harbor in December 1941. Their task was to infiltrate the harbor and sink the stationary American battle fleet. None succeeded, and all five were destroyed. The Japanese navy pinned great hopes on this type of submarine and built them in vast quantities. In fact, few opportunities for their use ever emerged, and they proved an expensive distraction.

Midget Submarines

he only way to sink ships berthed in harbors or anchorages that were too shallow or too well defended to allow attack by full-sized submarines was through the use of Midget Submarines. There were three main types: the human torpedo, first developed by the Italians and known as the "Chariot" in British circles, which fixed a detachable warhead to its target; the British "X craft," a perfect submarine in miniature with detachable explosive charges; and the two-man, torpedo-firing submersible, developed by the Japanese and Germans. All Midget Submarines had a limited range and had to be transported to their target area by a mother submarine, which would then await their return. In fact, very few crews were ever recovered. They knew that many were setting out on a one-way mission, the end result of which would be capture—or death.

SUCH LITTLE SPACE

Space inside this miniature submarine was so cramped that there was only room for one of the four crew to stretch out and sleep. Food was cooked over a tiny Bunsen burner stove, and there was a primitive toilet. This lock-in/lock-out compartment allowed the diver to leave the submarine to clear obstructions and plant limpet mines if required

THE AMERICAN X-2

Not to be left out of the miniature arms race, the U.S. Navy began experimenting with different designs. One such experiment was with this Fairchild-built torpedo-firing Midget Submarine. However, while these tests were being carried out, bigger submarines had already done the job.

MOBILE MIDGETS

The introduction of the German midget submarine "Bibel" was an attempt to stave off the Allied invasion of Europe. A miniature U-boat fleet of about 390 craft was built. All of the designs had an underslung torpedo and were highly mobile. Like the Japanese, German strategists misused their Midget Submarines by attempting to employ them in orthodox submarine roles. Their true, and only, strength was against a static and landlocked target.

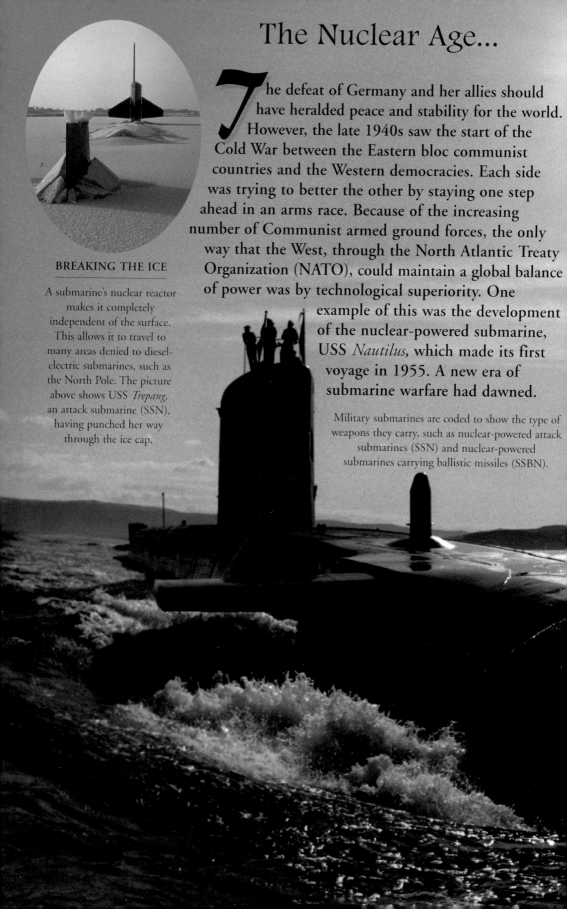

The Nuclear Age...

*T*he defeat of Germany and her allies should have heralded peace and stability for the world. However, the late 1940s saw the start of the Cold War between the Eastern bloc communist countries and the Western democracies. Each side was trying to better the other by staying one step ahead in an arms race. Because of the increasing number of Communist armed ground forces, the only way that the West, through the North Atlantic Treaty Organization (NATO), could maintain a global balance of power was by technological superiority. One example of this was the development of the nuclear-powered submarine, USS *Nautilus*, which made its first voyage in 1955. A new era of submarine warfare had dawned.

Military submarines are coded to show the type of weapons they carry, such as nuclear-powered attack submarines (SSN) and nuclear-powered submarines carrying ballistic missiles (SSBN).

BREAKING THE ICE

A submarine's nuclear reactor makes it completely independent of the surface. This allows it to travel to many areas denied to diesel-electric submarines, such as the North Pole. The picture above shows USS *Trepang*, an attack submarine (SSN), having punched her way through the ice cap.

SURVEILLANCE

As HMS *Conqueror* demonstrated during the Falklands War in 1982, it is possible for any nuclear-powered submarine to operate unsupported many thousands of miles from base. The only limiting factor for endurance is the amount of food it can carry. This periscope camera panoramic sweep shows the SSN's capability to conduct surveillance operations of a potential enemy's coastline.

KEEPING THE CREW HAPPY

Since crews of nuclear-powered submarines spend many months on patrol, out of touch with their families, great effort is made to look after their morale. Food is an important factor, and catering is therefore of the highest quality. Expert cooks ensure that there is always a meal available. When the modern submariner is not on watch helping with the routine operation of the submarine, or completing the inevitable paperwork, he will relax by listening to music or watching movies, of which there is always a plentiful supply.

HIDE AND SEEK

Britain's first Polaris-missile-equipped SSBN, HMS *Resolution*, is shown on passage down the River Clyde heading for its patrol area. The *Resolution*'s main task on patrol was to remain hidden.

...The Nuclear Age

The Soviet Union exploded its first nuclear bomb in 1949, and within a year of USS *Nautilus* going to sea, Moscow introduced its first operational nuclear-powered submarine. Thus, in the late 1950s, the temperature of the Cold War was distinctly frosty and the balance of military power apparently lay with the Soviet-dominated Warsaw Pact. A correction was needed by the West, and this arrived in 1960 with the launch of a Polaris ballistic missile by USS *George Washington*. This event had a huge political and military impact since, for the first time, it was possible to attack enemy lands from a submerged submarine secure from discovery or attack. The world had changed forever.

INTERCONTINENTAL COOPERATION

Britain's first nuclear-powered submarine, HMS *Dreadnought*, was launched in 1960. The decision for the Royal Navy to enter the nuclear age was taken by Earl Mountbatten, the First Sea Lord. It was a decision greatly welcomed by the United States, who provided *Dreadnought* with its nuclear reactor to help get it to sea as soon as possible. Since then the two navies have worked very closely together, with Britain adopting similar weapon systems and strategies to that of its more powerful ally. HMS *Vanguard*, a Trident missile submarine, is a current example of that cooperation.

THE NUCLEAR REACTOR

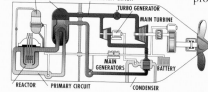

The process of nuclear fission that takes place inside a nuclear reactor produces a vast amount of heat, which boils water into steam. This then drives two main engines for propulsion and two turbogenerators for electrical power.

EVER-READY SUBMARINES

At its height, the U.S. Navy's Polaris force consisted of over 40 submarines, of which roughly half would be on patrol at any one time. These formidable submarines weighed over 8,000 tons and carried 16 missiles, each with a range of 2,500 miles. The British Royal Navy's *Resolution* Class submarines were very similar in size and shape. Their job at sea was to be in a position to respond instantly to any preemptive strike against a NATO country.

THE TOTEM POLE

The totem pole was the mascot of HMS *Totem*, a submarine from an earlier generation. It still stands as a continuing symbol of the submarine as a hunter. During the Cold War, Western SSNs monitored the whereabouts of Soviet nuclear submarines. They also acted as the first line of defense for aircraft carrier battle fleets and friendly SSBNs in the cat and mouse game of war beneath the sea.

CRUISE MISSILES

In the early 1990s another capability was added to *Los Angeles* Class SSNs with the fitting of vertical-launched Tomahawk cruise missiles. This inertial-guided missile can be fired against land or ship targets out to ranges in excess of 2,000 miles. It is guided by a map in its memory against land targets, and flies at a very low level. It came to prominence during the Gulf War against Iraq when a reporter from CNN watched one fly past his hotel window!

BACK TO BASE

In addition to providing facilities for rest (a comfortable bed) and recreation (opportunities for sport) for crews when they return from patrol, the submarine's base also houses workshops and medical facilities. Between patrols, the crew have an opportunity to spend time with their families, as well as repairing machinery to prepare the submarine for its next commitment. Refreshed and repaired, both crew and machine will be ready once again for many weeks or months at sea.

SEAL DELIVERY VEHICLE

The modern equivalent for landing special forces such as the American SEALS is the U.S. Navy's Mk VIII Delivery Vehicle. Like World War II's Chariots, the Swimmer Delivery Vehicle is carried by a mother submarine to the vicinity of the target objective. The great advantage of the combination is that the SEAL team is landed in total secrecy—without being exhausted by having to paddle for miles!

THE GREAT SUBMARINE RACE

The two biggest surface navies in the world belong to the United States and Russia who have the greatest number of submarines. Other nations that operate nuclear-powered submarines and possess ballistic missiles are China, Britain, and France. Many more countries operate diesel-electric submarines, with new entries including Iran and, in the near future, Malaysia.

MODERN CONDITIONS

Whatever the nationality, life at sea in a submarine is not comfortable, but at least today it is tolerable. The two sailors in their bunks show how crowded living spaces are, and how necessary it is for the submariner to get along with fellow crew members! The bunk is the only "private" space available, demonstrated by the young sailor writing a letter home.

UP-TO-DATE MACHINES

The modern diesel-electric submarine can vary in size from almost 3,000 tons down to 450 tons. The submarine pictured belongs to the Japanese Maritime Defense Force, which operates about 16 of them in two flotillas at Kure and Yokosuka. They are highly capable, being fitted with the latest in sonar technology and armed with long-range torpedoes and Sub-Harpoon radar homing antiship missiles. They carry 20 weapons and have a top speed of 20 knots when submerged. They are manned by a crew of 75.

ENDURANCE AT SEA

One of the great demands on the submarine is that it remains at sea for long periods, often far from base. It is essential therefore that it can take care of itself so that it does not have to keep rushing back to harbor for repairs. For example, the diving team on board can fix irritating external rattles!

INTERIOR DESIGNS

The interior of this French nuclear-powered ballistic missile submarine shows how big they have become! There are now three decks to negotiate, with masses of machinery as far as the eye can see. Crew size is about 120. The French submarine force is a powerful one with six SSBNs, six SSNs, and seven diesel-electric submarines. Their attack submarines (SSNs) have a speed of 25 knots.

SEA MONSTERS

The Russian *Typhoon* SSBN, weighing 26,000 tons when submerged, is the largest submarine ever built. It is 1,880 feet (562 meters) long, and carries 20 ballistic missiles, each with 6–9 warheads each. In addition to the *Typhoon*, Russia has *Delta* Class SSBNs, and was expected to maintain an operational force of about 25 of them. The Russian navy also has about 50 SSNs, some with anti-land-cruise-missile capability, and 40 diesel electric submarines, but economic problems now keep many of the Russian submarines at their base instead of on patrol.

Submarines Today

Politically and economically, the world is an ever-changing place. Since the fall of the Berlin Wall there have been a number of treaty realignments in Europe. In addition, particularly in East Asia and South America, we have seen the emergence of what were formerly "developing" countries as powerful economies. What remains unchanged is the total reliance on the sea by maritime nations for the transport of their export merchandise and import of essential raw materials. Indeed, since 1950, because of the growth of container traffic, seaborne trade has increased twelvefold. For maritime nations the interruption of this trade would threaten their economic survival. So it is vital for world stability that international shipping routes are kept free and open, and this can only be achieved by the protection of well-trained naval forces. Submarines in the hands of an aggressor could be used with devastating effect against harbors and merchant shipping. Many countries, conscious of the lessons of history, are now adding submarines to their navies as a deterrent to potential foes.

DEEP SEA EXPLORATION

The oil industry has benefited a great deal from the ability of submarines to lay and inspect pipelines—potentially avoiding major pollution threats to the oceans. Submarines have also helped scientists to explore the deepest parts of the world's oceans, photographing and investigating shipwrecks such as that of the *Titanic*.

DID YOU KNOW?

The first submarine to dive beyond its limits—and survive—was the USS *Porpoise* in 1903. The crew definitely had a salty sea story to tell when they finally made it back to the surface! They sank by accident to 130 feet, well beyond the depth for which the submarine was built. To make matters worse, the compressed air that should have raised their craft to the surface failed, so they had to use hand pumps to empty water from the submarine. Fortunately their efforts were not in vain; the only damage done was to pride and a few rivets!

In 1925 pigeons were used for communicating with shore from underwater. Pigeons were already used to pass messages from surfaced submarines, but the Japanese navy took it one step further. A report in the *Osaka Mainichi* newspaper told of an experiment whereby a pigeon, placed in a watertight container, had been ejected to the surface via a torpedo tube. When the container, which took two minutes for its journey, reached the surface, its cap blew off and the pigeon flew away, successfully delivering the message. The Japanese pigeon population greatly welcomed the introduction of wireless equipment!

Early antisubmarine experiments involved two sea lions. Before the introduction of ASDIC (known as sonar), there was no way of detecting a submarine other than the naked eye. In 1917 the British Royal Navy attempted to train two sea lions in the art of submarine detection. They were called Queenie and Billikins, and reacted well at first to the tasty morsels of fish that were offered as incentives. Unfortunately, Billikins ruined the experiment because he consistently preferred the company of bathers in Stokes Bay, a beach close to his training ground!

The submarine was introduced into the British Royal Navy in the face of violent opposition. In 1900 the submarine was regarded by the navy as the weapon of a weak power, and was described as "underhand, underwater, and damned un-English." Being a submariner was also regarded as "no occupation for a gentleman," and submariners were referred to by their contemporaries as "unwashed chauffeurs." They would soon get respect!

The Russian-built *Typhoon* is the biggest submarine ever built. This monster submarine of 27,000 tons is almost the length of two soccer fields. It is made up of two standard hulls of ordinary submarines joined together, and carries 20 intercontinental ballistic missiles with a range of 4,500 miles. The conning tower is so high that the personnel on the bridge can look down on sailors on a destroyer alongside.

The inventor of the locomotive torpedo, Sir Robert Whitehead, was the great-grandfather of the Austrian Von Trapp Singers of the film *The Sound of Music* fame. Sir Robert was working for the Austrian government when he stunned the world with his invention. His granddaughter, Frances, a lady of great beauty, married a future Austrian submarine ace, Captain Georg Von Trapp, in 1912. Frances died of scarlet fever after having a family of five children, and they formed the nucleus of the singing group. Maria, the young novice nun who became the second wife of Von Trapp, also had children, and they completed the famous songsters. It was because of Captain Von Trapp's submarine background that he was sought after by the Nazis.

ACKNOWLEDGMENTS

We would like to thank: Graham Rich, Hazel Poole, and Tina Chambers for their assistance. Picture research by Image select.

First Edition for the United States, Canada, and the Philippines published by Barron's Educational Series, Inc., 1998

First published in Great Britain in 1998 by ticktock Publishing Ltd., The Office, The Square, Hadlow, Kent, TN11 0DD, United Kingdom, in association with the British Royal Navy Submarine Museum

Copyright ©1998 ticktock Publishing Ltd.

All inquiries should be addressed to: Barron's Educational Series, Inc.
250 Wireless Boulevard, Hauppauge, New York 11788
http://www.barronseduc.com

Library of Congress Catalog Card No. 98-70732

International Standard Book Number 0-7641-0536-1

Printed in Italy

Picture Credits: t=top, b=bottom, c=center, l=left, r=right
AKG (London): 9l. Ancient Art & Architecture: OFC & 2/3c. Ann Ronan (@ Image Select: 5tr, 6c, 6cb, OFC & 8tl. Corbis/Everett: 3tl. Giraudon: 23c. Image Select: 9tr. Jim Sugar Photography/Corbis: 29br. Lawson Wood/Corbis: 31tr. National Maritime Museum: OFC(main photograph), OFC & 7br, OFC & 18/19c. Pix: 30bl. Royal Navy Submarine Museum: IFC/1, 2br, 3tr, 5tl, 4l, OFC & 4bl, 5cb, 6tl, 7tr, 8/9c, 9tl, 9br, 9tr, OBC & 10/11c, 13br, 12tl, 12cb, 11cl, 14tl, 14bl, 15tl, 16l, 16tl, 16tr, 19bl, 19br, 20tl, 20c, 21bl, 21tl, 23tl, 23br, 24l, 25b, 27tl, 26/27, OBC & 28tl. Stuart Westmorland/Corbis: 2tl. UPI/Corbis-Bettmann: 15c. U.S. Department of Defense/Corbis: 26tl, 30r. Yogi inc/Corbis: 18tl, 21tr, 27tr, 29c, 29tr, 30tr, 30c, 31b.

Every effort has been made to trace the copyright holders and we apologize in advance for any unintentional omissions. We would be pleased to insert the appropriate acknowledgment in any subsequent edition of this publication.

BARRON'S